Dog Tails

Rachel Davies

BookLeaf
Publishing

India | USA | UK

Presentation by *BookLeaf Publishing*

Web: www.bookleafpub.com

E-mail: info@bookleafpub.com

ISBN: 9789358315455

First edition 2022

DEDICATION

Dedicated to all those dog's I've loved but who are now over rainbow bridge, with special mention to:

Bunny

Binxy

Boris

ACKNOWLEDGEMENT

Acknowledging my mum, the woman who gave me the confidence to speak my mind, to ask a thousand questions and who encouraged my passion of reading and writing.

To James Smith for all his help with the artwork.

Also to Mark Davies my husband and Packleader, for humouring me and for loving me even when I'm annoying.

PREFACE

I spend my days in the company of dogs, all different breeds and temperaments. Their behaviour and quirks inspired me to write these poems. Many life lessons can be taken from dogs - always sniff food before you eat it, take the opportunity to pee when you can even if you don't really need to go, love unconditionally and take naps!

My Dog

My dog does not mind if my hair is a mess,
If my make up isn't perfect, he couldn't care
less!
My dog never tells me I look fat in my dress
We wear matching bows when we want to
impress!

My dog looks at me with pure love in his eyes
Unlike some men he never lies!
My dog loves me of this I'm sure
He always waits outside the bathroom door.

My dog takes up a lot of the bed
His paw on occasion kicking my head.
My dog likes to share my meals
On occasion a Malteser he steals!

My dog saves me from anyone who looks shady
He alerts me to the wind, the postman, and the
Avon lady.
My dog is my protector he does not waiver
He is my superhero and greatest saviour.

I Don't Like It

I don't like it when you take me to the vet
Or when you bath me and I'm wet.
I don't like it when you are gone all day
Nor when you yell at me to get out the way!

I don't like it when you give me healthy treats
Give me pigs ears and chicken feet!
I don't like it when you are sad
Even worse if you are mad.

I don't like thunder nor fireworks night
Loud sounds you see give me a fright.
I don't like walking in the rain and snow
Out with you I will not go.

I don't like when it's too hot, keep me cool
hydrated and fill up the paddling pool.
I don't like it when you give other dogs attention
I want you to show only me affection.

I do like giving my mates bums a sniff
It's information city when I get a whiff.
I do like belly scratches and ear rubs galore
And cuddles with you I always want more.

Dog Jobs

Rottweilers and Dobermans are loyal
Whereas Shih-Tzus are just royal.
If you have food Labradors have your attention
And Cockapoos just want affection.

Frenchie's snort and fart
Border Collies, well they are smart.
Dogs such as the Afghan Hound
Are considered the silliest around.

Great Danes like scooby snacks
Police dogs are trained to attack.
Terriers are built to hunt rats and mice
And Cavaliers are sweet and nice.

Retrievers bring back balls you have thrown in
the park
German Shepherds at intruders bark.
Whippets and Greyhounds are built for speed
Whereas some dogs just dig up weeds.

Working Cocker Spaniels are just nuts
And Dalmatians like models simply strut.
Mastiffs were some of the Roman dogs of war
Whereas some dogs just scratch at your door.

Dogs distant relative the wolf is where they descend from
They came near the fires where cavemen sat on their bum.
From the fearsome wolf with teeth and straggly hair
We now have our best friends that sleep in our chair

.

Squirrels

Squirrels are simply the best thing to try to catch
Their speed however I cannot match.
They always scurry up a tree
And then they get away from me.

After this the squirrels I never can seem to find
It drives me crazy and out of my mind.
Those squirrels they like to taunt
Their furry tails I swear they flaunt.

I snort and bark, but it does not matter
Those squirrels just seem to scatter.
Red, grey, or black squirrels are the best
Until I catch one, I will not rest.

Legend has it a dog caught a squirrel one time
Because up a tree it did not climb.
The squirrel gave a nasty scratch to its nose
So now that dog chases crows.

Disgusting Dogs

My humans love me with all their heart
Perhaps a little less when I do a stinky fart.
My breath smells after I've eaten tripe
And across the carpet my bum I wipe.

Sometimes I eat others dogs sick
and my privates I often lick.
I like to eat duck and geese poo
Or deposit my own in a shoe.

I love jumping in muddy puddles
Then trying to give you lots of cuddles.
I will hunt rats and mice
Sometimes I'll come home with lice.

I like drinking water out the loo
Or better than that rolling in fox poo.
Sometimes I'll slobber and it will land on the
wall
Or I'll lean on your lap and just drawl.

I like to sniff other dogs bums
It's how I make my chums!
Sometimes I will chew a dirty sock
I once pee'd up a lady's frock.

I will lick your sweat when you've been to the
gym
I know my activities might seem grim.
I'm sorry if this causes you distress
But my behaviour is up to you to address.

Therapy Dogs

When people are sick in their hospital bed
I let them stroke and pet my head.
I often visit the old peoples home
It helps them feel not so alone.

I'm there to ease grief on dark days
My presence can help in so many ways.
I'm here if you just need somebody near
Or when an appointment strikes you with fear.

I'm happy to hear you talk
Or with you I'll quietly walk.
I can help ease that tension
When it's just too hard to mention.

My purpose you see is to help humankind
When things are heavy and trouble their mind.
Some say I might be God's best creation
A pure sole that brings salvation

Rescued

Please bear with me I have some baggage to
unpack
I was found with my siblings tied up in a sack.
We were fished out the water, a kind man pulled
us out
Without his help we would have died no doubt.

I don't recall my mother, we must have been
separated at birth
But here I am on this green planet we call earth.
We were all dried off, checked over and fed
We all then slept soundly in a warm comfy bed.

There's another dog at this house
He's as quiet as a church mouse.
He doesn't like it if you stroke his head
His old owner beat him until almost dead.

These are woeful stories I'm telling you
Dogs so nervous if you just say boo.
Dogs that were tied up and forgot
Dogs left in abandoned houses to rot.

Dogs left on the corner of the street
Some dogs who have sores upon their feet.
Some dogs thrown from cars into the road
All by people with no moral code.

So thanks to those humans who give us time to
unwind
To let us decompress the demons in our mind.
Here's to those who volunteer
To those who make us feel safe with nothing to
fear.

Day Care Dogs

There's Bert and Bess rolling around on the
floor
And Beau alerting me to someone at the door.
There's always Loki looking for a treat
Or Molly who likes to hump my feet.

Some dogs are hiding, namely Mabel
Usually, with a bone under the table.
There's Milo the old boy curled up in the corner
And Poppy by the fireplace just getting warmer.

Winnie is giving me soulful looks with her eyes
Otto's peed on the rug what a surprise!
Barney and Betsy are fighting for my lap.
And there's Luna obsessed with the cat.

Beckett is a princess with a bow in her hair
For other dogs she does not care.
Shadow, Henley and Charlie make quite the trio
Then there's mad as a hatter Leo.

There's Dory and Rae Rae the adorable pugs
Alice a police dog who can sniff out drugs.
Willow, Peggy, and Sally too
These are the day-care dogs to name but a few.

Cats Vs Dogs

Dogs are always happy to greet you with a
waggy tail and a lick
Just grateful to live in the moment with a stick.
Cats however couldn't care less
Cats just want humans to clean up their mess.

Dogs are easier to train
Cats just look at you with disdain.
Cats will knock objects of the tabletop
Whereas dogs have cute noses to bop.

Dogs will eat anything at feeding time
Cats won't touch it unless gourmet and sublime.
Cats will cough up furballs on your clean sheets
But dogs you can take for a walk on the streets.

Some dogs help the deaf and blind
Most cats are busy licking their behind.
Cats act like they are the best thing since sliced
bread
But you can teach a dog tricks like how to play
dead.

Cats will meow at you in the middle of the night
Or jump on you to give you a fright.
Dogs will save you from a thief
And lick your tears if you feel grief.

Boris

My old boys muzzle grew grey
We knew it was time to call it a day.
His eyes grew heavy, his breathing wasn't so
good
He wasn't drinking or walking like he should.

It was a hard choice to make
I thought my heart would break.
I had him since he was 8 weeks old
In his youth he was big, brash, and bold.

His stature was impressive, his head large
Weighing 84 kilos and built like a barge.
He liked to chase the lady dogs you see
And on every lamppost, he would pee.

He did the stinkiest loudest farts
But took up the biggest place in my heart.
Everyone loved him when they met him in the
park.
He would sometimes scare people in the dark.

He lived such a pure long life
Gave me little trouble or strife.
He was my fearless companion right to the end
My handsome boy my best friend.

The Vet

The vet checked me over said I'd put on weight well
We can all blame Pavlov who rang a bell!
Next he checked my microchip was in place
He gave me a pat, said what a cute face.

Then the vet gave me a jab
He sent my bloods off to the lab.
Collected my pee in a cup
Results say I'm a healthy pup.

I overheard him say I'm fully vaccinated
Then they mentioned about getting me castrated.
I'm not really sure what this may mean
But to be honest I'm not really keen.

The vets is a scary place I fear
So hold me close and near.
I don't look forward to my visits here
Let me make that perfectly clear.

The New Arrival

The humans have multiplied
This kid has been nine months inside.
It cries all night and always wants to be fed
Excuse me while I go back to bed.

A lot of visitors have come to see
This tiny pink new-born baby.
I barked when they arrived
And then when they came inside.

I used to be their only focus point
Now this baby is stinking up the joint.
It crawls around and tries to tug my tail
I try to get away, to no avail.

I do consider this kid part of my pack
The humans have this family on track.
I make sure that he's tucked in tight
I like to sleep in his room at night.

I'll be honest I've taken a shine
This kid of theirs, well he's now mine.
Best friends we have become
But he's theirs when he has a pooey bum.

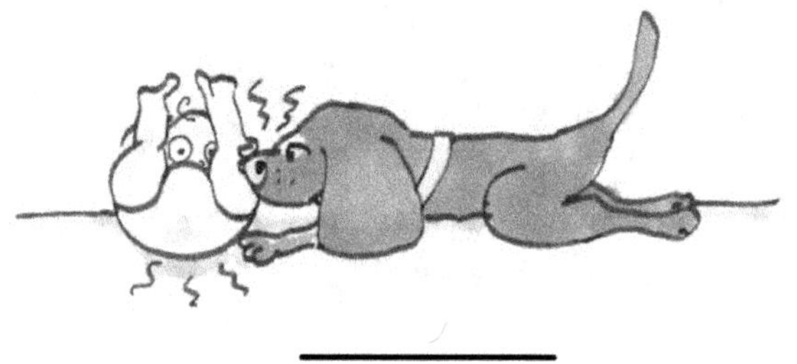

I'm Bored

I can't do a puzzle or play an X-box game
Without a walk the day feels the same
When you are tired from being at work all day
Make some time for me and play.

When I was little, you played with me a lot
Now I'm grown up you seem to have forgot.
Please don't make me sit here all alone
While you scroll for hours on your phone.

We could go to the beach
Or new tricks you could teach.
We could go for a ride in the car
Anywhere really it needn't be far.

You could take me to a dog friendly place to eat
We could get some snacks for me as a treat.
We could schedule some play dates
With some of my best doggy mates.

Keep my mind and body exercised.
Even the vet of this advised.
When I'm tired and ready to call it a night
I'll sit on your lap and you can hold me tight.

Famous Dogs

When we think about our canine counterparts
There are those that steal our hearts.
Childhood friends such as Snoopy
Or that great cartoon detective Droopy.

Dogs have been in the movies and the news
Some dogs do more than just chew shoes.
What about Laika who went into space
or Hooch who had slobber all over his face.

Lady and the Tramp shared a spaghetti dinner
There's Pudsey a Britain's Got Talent winner.
When the world cup got stolen and went astray
A dog called Pickles found it and saved the day.

Bullseye is famous in Oliver Twist by Dickens
Or Cujo the film by Stephen King sickens.
There's Clifford the big dog that's red
In Marley and me we all cried when he was
dead.

There's Lassie who found Tim down the well
And Pavlov's dog who responded to a bell.
All these amazing dogs we know from history
Most famous of all is Scooby always solving the
mystery!

The Importance Of Food

What we feed our dogs really does matter
If you feed rubbish their poo will go splatter.
Food that is high in an e-number
Won't help your dog get a good night's slumber.

The idea of just feeding scraps is outdated
The behaviour of dogs and food intake is related.
In the shops there's a huge variety
For your dog's needs that are dietary.

There's food that's complete and raw
Food to strengthen your dogs jaw.
Certain high energy dog treats
Has the same effect as kids eating Haribo
sweets.

It's always best to invest
In the food that your dog will digest.
Ensure your dog gets all the nutrients they need
In the food with which you feed.

The Dirty Dog

I went to the groomers because I was scruffy
With shampoo and conditioner they made me
fluffy.
The very next day I played in the mud
Mums jaw dropped open with a thud.

Another clean-up is needed she said
Before you can sleep up on my bed.
She ordered me up the stairs and into the bath
No way, not again you're having a laugh!

The dirt came off in the tub
My tail got an extra scrub.
I thought to myself I know what to do
The very next day I rolled in fox poo.

Mum seemed kind of mad
Yelled at me for being bad.
I was subjected to another clean
Why are these humans just so mean?

Ugh who
was that

Some Dogs

Some dogs pull on the lead
Dragging their owner at breakneck speed.
Some dogs if they see a hoover will make a fuss
Equally so if they see a red double decker bus.

Some dogs jump up
Knocking the coffee out of your cup.
Some dogs are terrified of the mop or broom
Or some don't like it when a car goes zoom.

Some dogs go berserk when squirrels are sighted
Or if a guest arrives gets over excited.
Some dogs hate the rain
You see the sound is magnified causing pain.

Some dogs want to chase cats
Some dogs growl at men wearing hats.
Some dogs dig up flowers and the ground
Some dogs bark continuously making your head
pound.

Some dogs want to fight other dogs they see
Some dogs in the house they pee.
Some dogs chew the skirting board
Others take their bones and hoard.

All of the above can be effectively addressed
With patients and training who'd have guessed?
Take the time to invest in your dog and best
friend
It will make for a happier household in the end.

Beach Days

My dog likes to scruff up and dig in the sand
Or roll on his back like he's getting tanned.
He likes to eat the seaweed washed up on the
ocean shaw
Or chase the seagulls as they cry "gaw gaw"

I let him share my ice cream cone
He chases the pebbles I have thrown.
He sniffs the dead fish that washed up on the
beach
Eating these is bad I try to teach.

He paddles in the warm sea getting wet
He stood on a jelly fish that cost him the vet.
He likes to chase the ball along the smooth sand
He brings it back for the treat in my hand.

A day at the beach with my dog leaves me
shattered
But he's had a great time and that's what
mattered.
And now we are home it's time to rest
Beach days with my dog are simply the best.

Things Dogs Teach Us

Dogs don't hold a grudge they move on
On negative thoughts they don't spend long.
If they don't like something they walk away
And as long as they have been for a walk it's
been a good day.

They teach us love is unconditional
And to always accept snacks that are additional.
They don't dwell they live in the moment
Teaching us communication in a relationship is a
key component.

They teach us to love freely and hard
And sometimes we needn't look further than our
own backyard.
They teach us to enjoy the simple things is life
And starting fights only causes strife.

They teach us resting is good for the soul
And eight hours a day is the goal.
They teach us to stand up for our mates
And that we all have our own skills and traits.

Perhaps dogs best teaching
Is best friend bonds are far reaching.
Living a life that's not complicated
Can leave you feeling pretty elated.

So God Made A Dog

God said I need someone willing to sit and wait
To be humans' friend and best mate.
Someone with no ego who doesn't judge
Someone when the chips are down doesn't
budge.

A creature to love unconditionally and
completely
And to love humans ever so sweetly.
A creation to bark when the door goes
An invention to take away woes.

Something who can help when humans are
stressed
For times when they are sad or depressed.
Someone to listen with an open ear
Or to keep us company while we drink beer.

For God spelt backwards is dog don't you see
That isn't a huge coincidence to me!
God invented the best creature for when he
couldn't be there.
Even before he knew it, he was answering a
prayer.

The Hardest Bit

The hardest bit isn't training your pup to do
what's right
Or waking up to let them out in the night.
It's not clearing up diarrhea that's runny
Trust me poo on your shoes isn't funny.

It's not hard to take them to puppy class
Or training them to pee on grass.
It's not difficult getting them to sit and wait
Or remembering to close the garden gate.

It's not too much of a task after a long day
To take them out for a run and play.
It's not too much bother feeding them right
Watching their weight and keeping them lite.

It's so quick to give them a shower
Or to re plant those dug up flowers.
It's no headache to brush their hair
For these dogs we deeply care.

The challenging bits are watching them shiver
with cold
Watching them get sicker, grey and old.
The hardest part is saying goodbye to your
friend
The hardest part is always the end.